Rourke
28.50

Full Throttle

Jeep

Tracy Maurer

Rourke
Publishing LLC
Vero Beach, Florida 32964

www.rourkepublishing.com

We recognize that some words, model names and designations, for example, mentioned herein are the property of the trademark holder. We use them for identification purposes only. This is not an official publication.

PHOTO CREDITS: Courtesy of the Library of Congress: pages 4 (bottom), 5 (top), 7 (inset), 8; Courtesy of DaimlerChrysler: all other images

AUTHOR CREDITS:
The author gratefully acknowledges project assistance provided by Tristan Roux at MN-Forum.com.

Also, the author extends appreciation to Mike Maurer, Lois M. Nelson, Margaret and Thomas, and the team at Rourke.

Editor: Robert Stengard-Olliges
Cover Design: Todd Field
Page Design: Nicola Stratford

Library of Congress Cataloging-in-Publication Data

Maurer, Tracy, 1965-
 Jeep / Tracy Nelson Maurer.
    p. cm. -- (Full throttle)
 Includes bibliographical references and index.
 ISBN 1-60044-223-4 (hardcover)
 ISBN 978-1-60044-363-3 (paperback)
 1. Jeep automobile--Juvenile literature. I. Title. II. Series: Maurer, Tracy, 1965-. Full throttle.
 TL215.J44M38 2006
 629.222'2--dc22   2006017519

Printed in the USA

CG/CG

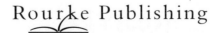

Rourke Publishing

www.rourkepublishing.com – sales@rourkepublishing.com
Post Office Box 3328, Vero Beach, FL 32964

Table of Contents

America's Victory Mobile

In 1903, the first newfangled Model A cars rumbled out of Henry Ford's factory. Just two years later, U.S. Army Captain William A. Phillips suggested a far-fetched (or far-sighted) idea: let's build a war car.

It seems nothing happened. Maybe the idea was too crazy. Cars weren't reliable in those days. Many people thought they were a fad. Although Captain Phillip's early war car idea didn't *look* like a jeep, his plan was amazingly similar to the actual 1940s vehicle.

The military jeep didn't come from just one person's idea. It didn't even come from just one company. In 1940, the U.S. Army wrote a wish-list for a lightweight, quarter-ton **4x4** *vehicle and asked 135 companies to send concepts. Only three delivered: Ford Motor Company, American Bantam Car Company, and Willys-Overland Motors.*

4x4
a vehicle that moves by a system that can send power to all four wheels

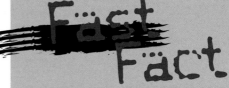

For a while, the U.S. Army seriously considered a motorcycle with a sidecar as an alternative to the jeep

Each company offered ideas that made the war jeep.
- Bantam: Compact shape and light weight.
- Ford: Slatted grille, flat hood, and folding windshield.
- Willys-Overland: Powerful "Go-Devil" engine.

The Army settled on its new all-American military vehicle just in time. By December 1941, America joined the Allied Forces in World War II.

Rallying the Allies

Jeeps played an important part in helping the Allied Forces win World War II. The German and Japanese enemies failed to build a car with as much off-road stability, speed, strength, and versatility. They tried to capture jeeps instead. American soldiers received instructions on how to smash, burn, blow up, and drown their jeeps to keep enemies from plundering the vehicles.

The Four-Wheeled Hero

Jeeps adapted easily to different tasks beyond ambulance, artillery, and troop transportation duty.
- "Waterproofed" jeeps swam through Italy's floods.
- Jeeps towed plows, hay trailers, and other farm equipment in England.
- Jeeps fitted with rail wheels pulled trains weighing up to 25 tons.

The Army jeep included a **jerry can**, axe, shovel, a machine gun mount, and blackout lighting—a hooded headlight that directs its

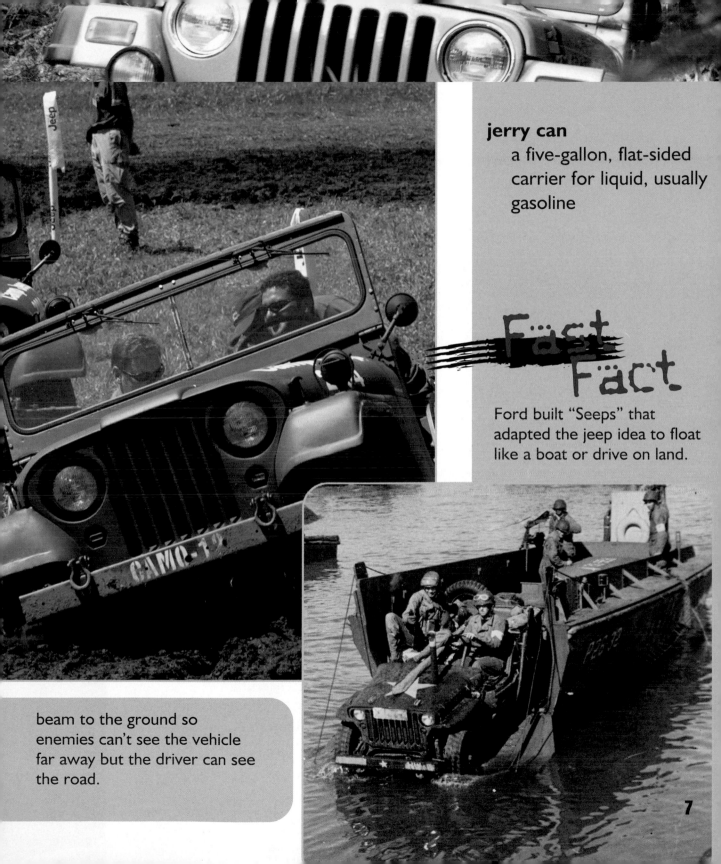

jerry can
    a five-gallon, flat-sided carrier for liquid, usually gasoline

Fast Fact

Ford built "Seeps" that adapted the jeep idea to float like a boat or drive on land.

beam to the ground so enemies can't see the vehicle far away but the driver can see the road.

Jeepers! What a Name

Where did the name come from? Between 1914 and 1918, World War I soldiers called any new vehicle or soldier a "jeep." In the 1930s, **civilians** said "jeep" and "jeepers" for anything cool or amazing. Most likely, the Willys-Overland drivers called their vehicles "jeeps" to separate them from Fords during the early Army testing. Willys-Overland won the Army contract and claimed the name.

*A popular myth is that the army called the jeep a "General Purpose" vehicle, or GP, which morphed into "jeep." In truth, Ford—not the Army—labeled its jeeps with "GPW." G stood for government contract. P meant an 80-inch (2 m) **wheelbase**. W showed it had a Willys-Overland engine.*

Other Famous Jeeps Before the Jeep®

- 1936 - "Eugene the Jeep," a sweet creature, appeared with Popeye in cartoons drawn by E.C. Segar.
- 1937 - Officially named the B-17 in 1937, this important long-range bomber aircraft originally had the nickname "Jeep." It soon changed to "Flying Fortress."
- 1938 - Halliburton Oil Well Cementing Company built a four-wheel-drive van called a "Jeep."
- 1940 - Dodge built a half-ton 4x4 called a "Jeep." This was later called a "Peep." *No comment!*
- 1943 - Minneapolis Moline Power Implement Company built a "Jeep" farm tractor, which was turned into a military 4x4 vehicle during World War II.

civilians
   people who are not soldiers or police

wheelbase
   the distance between the front and rear axles

Today, Jeep® is a registered trademark and the exclusive property of DaimlerChrysler, which owns the Jeep brand. People still say "jeep"—lowercase j—to mean any lightweight 4x4 vehicle.

Civilian Sales Battles

A carmaker since 1908, Willys-Overland knew from experience that it needed to have a vehicle ready to sell to civilians before World War II ended. In 1944, the company started working on CJ-1 (Civilian Jeep, Model One) to sell to farmers. They also tried a sports car in 1948 called the Jeepster. Of all the early civilian models, the 1953 CJ-3B "Universal Jeep" first proved what civilians really wanted: a **street-legal**, off-road-ready vehicle.

The Willys Motors division of Kaiser tested a Forward Control (FC) 4x4 in 1956. Based on a CJ-5 chassis, the snub-nose cab had roomy hauling space behind it. Businesses took interest but sales lagged. Production ended in 1965.

Jeep Milestones

- **1940** – Willys-Overland developed the military Jeep, such as the heroic MB.
- **1945** – The civilian Jeep arrived, leading to the popular CJ-5s.
- **1947** – The Willys Jeep Truck appeared.
- **1962** – The Wagoneer SUV was introduced.
- **1986** – The Wrangler arrived.
- **2006** – The Wrangler and all Jeeps continued to appeal to off-roaders.

street-legal
a vehicle allowed to be driven on city streets because it meets the standards set by law

The 1953 CJ-3B Universal Jeep kept the flat fenders and short 80-inch (2 m) wheelbase of earlier models. More powerful engine options soon followed with the CJ-5 in 1954, including a diesel and a V-6.

The company built several different Jeep models based on the successful CJ chassis to try to attract more customers. Engineers also stretched their thinking with longer wheelbases. One of the leading ideas combined 4x4 power with a 110-inch (2.8 m) station-wagon design. The comfortable, family-styled 1962 Wagoneer was one of the earliest luxury SUVs.

The successful Wagoneer hinted at the SUV era ahead. The Grand Cherokee didn't replace the Wagoneer until 1993.

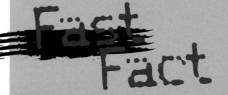

News reports showing tippy Jeep CJs in the 1980s were later questioned for not telling the full story. But the damage was done and CJ production ended in 1986.

The two-wheel-drive option never sold well for Jeep except to the U.S. Postal Service. They had steering wheels on the left or right side. Production ended in the 1980s, but many mail carriers still depend on them.

Wrangler Arrives

Hardcore off-roaders didn't take kindly to the end of CJs. Some people rushed to buy the last available CJ-7s and CJ-8s. They believed there wouldn't be another true Jeep. American Motor Corporation quickly introduced the Jeep Wrangler YJ. The new 4x4 squatted lower and wider than the old CJ for greater stability.

Wrangler looked a lot like the CJs—and still does. In time, Wrangler TJ built on the YJ's success. In 2003, the Wrangler Rubicon left no doubt that this Jeep line delivered the tough stuff.

Wrangler Rubicon is named for one of the most rugged off-road trails in the U.S. The 22-mile (35.5 km) Rubicon Trail twists and turns across the Sierra Nevada to Lake Tahoe.

Fast Fact.

Wranglers use part-time four-wheel drive. Drivers shift it into action as needed.

Like the early two-door Wranglers, today's version comes with part-time four-wheel drive. But buyers have more options than ever before. After the basic SE package, Wranglers come in X, Sport, Unlimited, Rubicon, and Unlimited Rubicon versions.

FROM: The base-line SE offers half metal doors and plastic windows in a soft top that doubles as the "air-conditioning" system when removed.

TO: The ready-to-rock Unlimited Rubicon comes with more off-road equipment, including locking **differentials** for better traction. It also packs in more creature-comforts than the shorter SE, such as roll-up windows, true air conditioning, and more backseat leg room.

differential
the device on each axle that sends power to the wheels and allows the axles to spin at different speeds; a locking differential makes sure the driven wheels turn at the same speed

Of all the modern Jeep models, the two-door Wrangler looks most like the original Jeep. It even has a fold-down windshield for off-road driving.

The Mighty Climber

The Unlimited Rubicon clears the ground by a full 10 inches (25.5 cm). It can handle a 44.9° **approach angle** and 33.9° **departure angle**—nearly matching the original World War II Jeep.

Wrangler shares the traditional boxy military shape and the slotted grille that traces its roots to the 1940s. Today, the entire Jeep line uses a seven—slotted grille.

Fast Fact

When climbing up or down, Wrangler's short 24-inch (61 cm) overhang lets it tackle steeper angles than 4x4s with longer, grille-grinding noses.

approach angle
    the steepest or highest angle a vehicle can start climbing a slope without damaging its front

departure angle
    the steepest or highest angle a vehicle can exit from a slope without damaging its rear

Jeep boasts a full list of safety features for Wranglers, including "rollover hoop protection" and airbags.

The Wrangler looks handsome heading off the highway—and coming back to it. That's because the diamond-plate sill guards and black rubber bumpers aren't just for style. They're handy dent-preventers for boulder-bashing trails.

17

Jeepers' Creepers

Jeepers care about speed. Mainly, these off-road Jeep drivers want to control how *slowly* they can crawl over tough terrain without killing the engine. To plow through deep snow, slog along rutted muddy paths, or climb up rocky hills, the Wrangler combines a powerful engine with a proven four-wheel-drive system.

Six Cylinders

With an **inline** six-cylinder power plant under the hood, the Unlimited Rubicon kicks out 190 horsepower. Buyers can choose a four-speed automatic or a six-speed manual transmission.

Tow Hooks

Sometimes the trail wins. Every Unlimited Rubicon has two front tow hooks and one rear hook. Drivers can also release the 4x4 system for safe towing.

inline
> in a motor, the cylinders are set in a line; each cylinder has a chamber that burns fuel

suspension
> in a vehicle, the system of shock absorbers, springs, and other parts between the wheel and frame designed to create a smooth ride and better control

An Unlimited Rubicon driver can shift to a low gear to decrease the engine's speed and use it to add four times more forward strength or torque.

*Today's Wrangler uses a **suspension** system that delivers superior wheel movement and a decent ride (passengers should still avoid sipping sodas on bumpy roads).*

Fast Fact

Wranglers are sure-footed with almost perfectly balanced weight: 51% front and 49% rear.

Tested for the Trail

Jeeps have helped pave the way for all SUVs. From the compact Wrangler to the super-sized Commander, today's Jeeps fit just about any off-roading or on-highway style. Some drivers won't ever pick mud and rocks from the grille, but they like knowing that they could go off-road. The Nevada Automotive Test Center worked with Jeep to develop a system for showing that a Jeep is truly ready to tackle the trail.

The hefty seven-passenger Commander passed the off-roading standards developed in Nevada. Looking like Wrangler's Big Daddy, Commander shares the Jeep family's boxy shape and seven-slot grille.

Off-Road Test Factors

- Ground clearance
- Traction
- Maneuverability
- Water fording
- Wheel articulation

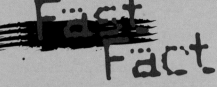
"HEMI" is the trademark for the DaimlerChrysler engine with hemispheric, or rounded, combustion cylinders.

Commander has more high-tech goodies than Wrangler, such as a backseat DVD player and a dashboard GPS (global positioning satellite) system.

Commander Engine

Under the hood, Commander's top option features a beastly V-8 HEMI® engine that rates 330 horsepower. It can tow a 3,000-pound (1,361 kg) trailer.

In 2005, Jeep paired a four-cylinder diesel engine option with its mid-size Liberty. Diesel engines can deliver decent power and good fuel economy. Grand Cherokee, the model between Liberty and Commander, skipped the diesel but added two hardy HEMI options—including one that's even bigger than Commander's.

The Jeep Compass first appeared at the 2002 North American International Auto Show. A boxier version hit showrooms by summer 2006.

Fast Fact

Outside of North America, Jeep sells the Liberty as the Cherokee.

Future Jeep Forecast

- Engines that produce more power and better fuel economy than today's engines
- Flexible interiors with many customizing options
- Improved four-wheel-drive and highway handling

Living Jeeply

Some Jeep owners take their Jeeps rather seriously, especially if they drive their Jeeps off-road. These jeepers see their Jeeps as more than transportation—the vehicles are an important part of their adventure lifestyle. Dents, crusty winches, and other clear signs of trail use mark their loyalty to the "Jeep Thing."

In 1952, long before all the SUV hoopla, Mark Smith gathered a few Jeep enthusiasts for a little drive along the Rubicon Trail. His annual trek has grown into Jeep Jamboree USA, a three-day four-wheeling event held at Rubicon and more than 30 other locations across America.

Fast Fact

At Jeep Jamboree USA, drivers learn how to safely enjoy off-road adventures.

CAMP JEEP

At Camp Jeep, Jeep owners talk directly to engineers. Their ideas (like round headlights) often show up in later models.

At Camp Jeep, the entire family discovers fun off-road activities. The Jeep-sponsored event emphasizes the Jeep as a way to enjoy driving and outdoor recreation, such as mountain-bike riding and fly-fishing.

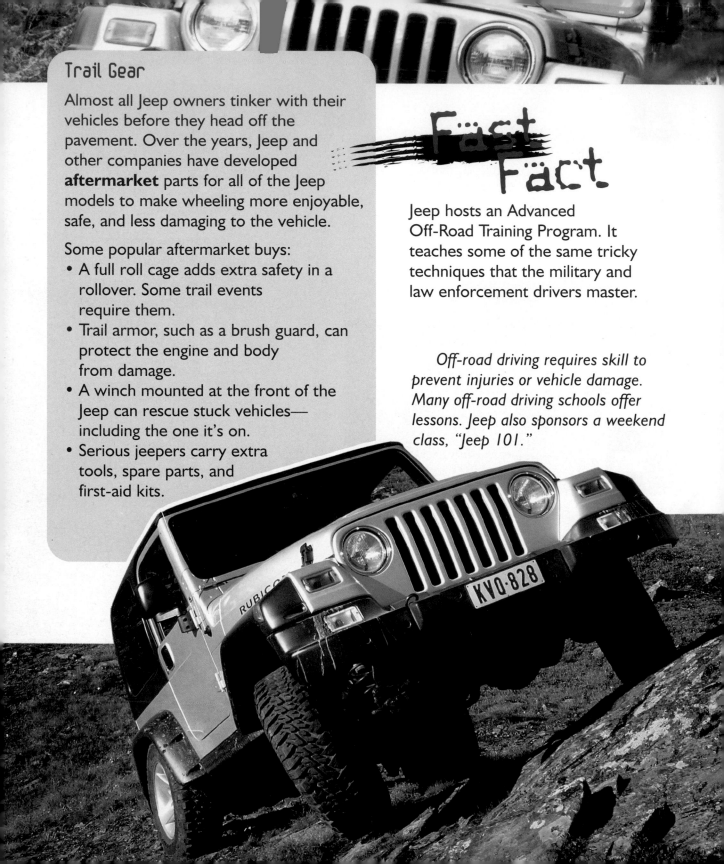

Trail Gear

Almost all Jeep owners tinker with their vehicles before they head off the pavement. Over the years, Jeep and other companies have developed **aftermarket** parts for all of the Jeep models to make wheeling more enjoyable, safe, and less damaging to the vehicle.

Some popular aftermarket buys:
- A full roll cage adds extra safety in a rollover. Some trail events require them.
- Trail armor, such as a brush guard, can protect the engine and body from damage.
- A winch mounted at the front of the Jeep can rescue stuck vehicles—including the one it's on.
- Serious jeepers carry extra tools, spare parts, and first-aid kits.

Fast Fact

Jeep hosts an Advanced Off-Road Training Program. It teaches some of the same tricky techniques that the military and law enforcement drivers master.

Off-road driving requires skill to prevent injuries or vehicle damage. Many off-road driving schools offer lessons. Jeep also sponsors a weekend class, "Jeep 101."

From ice racing in Colorado to mud bogging in Tennessee, if the event is off the pavement, then somebody's probably driving a Jeep there.

The 2006 Jeep Hurricane concept featured four-wheel steering.

Specially modified 4x4s, such as older CJ-7s and Wranglers, compete on nasty rock crawling courses. Drivers traverse gaping crevices and climb 60° walls. Four-wheel steering, tried long ago on the 1940 prototype jeep, has revived on rock-crawlers.

Where to Wheel

While Jeep has one of the most active company-sponsored off-road programs, many Jeepers chart their own adventures. Where do they go? Some public parks and trails allow 4x4 vehicles, such as Rubicon Trail in California and Moon Rocks in Reno, Nevada. Several clubs and organizations host rallies, treks, and competitions, too.

A few 4x4 favorites:
• Moab, Utah
• Hot Springs, Arkansas
• St. George, Utah
• Farmington, New Mexico
• Black Hills, South Dakota

Drivers should always check with local authorities for permission before launching down an unknown trail. All off-roaders should never leave anything more than their tread marks behind.

Some Jeep enthusiasts prefer old to new. **Restoration** work takes time, skill, and money to buy or make parts. A restored Jeep still has to comply with today's traffic laws. Restorers remove modern turn flashers and other street parts during competitions.

restoration
> to return something to
> its former condition

Fast Fact

Geocaching is (geography) +
caching (storing something).
It has become a popular
game worldwide.

Off-roaders have blended their
navigation skills and sense of
adventure into a global game called
"geocaching." They use their GPS
systems to follow clues at
geocaching.com to find hidden
rewards. Finders enter their visits
in logbooks and replace what they
find with new rewards.

Glossary

4x4 (FOR bih for) – a vehicle that moves by a system that can send power to all four wheels

aftermarket (AFF tur MAR kit) – parts added to a vehicle after its sale to the owner

approach angle (ah PROHCH ANG gl) – the steepest or highest angle a vehicle can start climbing a slope without damaging its front

civilians (si VILL yenz) – people who are not soldiers or police

departure angle (dee PAR chur ANG gl) – the steepest or highest angle a vehicle can exit from a slope without damaging its rear

differential (diff ah REN shul) – the device on each axle that sends power to the wheels and allows the axles to spin at different speeds; a locking differential makes sure the driven wheels turn at the same speed

inline (IN lihn) – in a motor, the cylinders are set in a line; each cylinder has a chamber that burns fuel

jerry can (JER ih kan) – a five-gallon, flat-sided carrier for liquid, usually gasoline

restoration (reh STOR ah shun) – to return something to its former condition

street-legal (STREET LEE gahl) – a vehicle allowed to be driven on city streets because it meets the standards set by law

suspension (sah SPEN shun) – in a vehicle, the system of shock absorbers, springs, and other parts between the wheel and frame designed to create a smooth ride and better control

wheelbase (WEEL bahs) – the distance between the front and rear axles

Further Reading

Ackerson, Robert. *Jeep CJ: 1945-1986*. Veloce Publishing, 2006.

Graham, Ian. *Off-Road Vehicles*. Heinemann Library, 2003.

Ludel, Moses. *Jeep Owner's Bible: A Hands-on Guide to Getting the Most from Your Jeep*. Bentley Publishers, 2004.

Maurer, Tracy Nelson. *Desert Racers*. Rourke Publishing, 2004.

Zaloga, Steven and Johnson, Hugh (illustrator). *Jeeps 1941-1945*. Osprey, 2005.

Websites

www.jeep.com

www.jeepforum.com

www.off-road.com

www.treadlightly.org

www.geocaching.com

Index

About the Author

Tracy Nelson Maurer writes nonfiction and fiction books for children, including more than 50 titles for Rourke Publishing LLC. Tracy lives with her husband Mike and two children near Minneapolis, Minnesota.